The Mark
of the Beast

Biblical answers for

you and your children

Michael S Fryer

Published by:
Father's House Congregation
Wales, UK

Edited by: Margaret Buckley

ISBN-13: 978-1541203914

For more information on the work of Michael Fryer, please visit:

www.FathersHouse.wales

Contents

Foreword

There are so many areas in Scripture which speak about the times in which we live. The ingathering of the Jews to the Land God promised to their forefathers is one major area of Scripture prophecy which is taking place in our lifetime.

This is so exciting and an amazing miracle, bearing in mind Jews have been persecuted in the nations for two thousand years and actually would have been destroyed if the nations had had their way.

The ingathering of The Jews to the land of Israel is as a sign to everyone that God is faithful to all His promises. How wonderful it is to see the words of so many prophets coming true in our lifetime. We are so privileged to be alive today to see the words of prophets such as Amos, who prophesied during the time of Jeroboam 786-746 BC, being fulfilled today in 2016.

The precise nature of the prophecies is also amazing, so much so that if you were to look at the prophecies concerning the birth, death and resurrection of Yeshua you would think that Prophets such as Isaiah and Zechariah were actually present when the events occurred.

There are 25 prophecies, given by the prophets, which give the exact details of the betrayal, trial, death and burial of Yeshua, all made between 1000 and 500 BC. The law of probabilities of these being fulfilled hundreds of years later in just a few short days shows us that it would have 1 in 33,554,432 chance of happening. The fact that it did happen says something about the accuracy of the prophecies in scripture.

Look for yourself at the following prophecies and compare them with the Gospel writer's accounts:

Psalm 22v7&8- He would be mocked.

Psalm 22v18- His garments would be parted.

Psalm 34v20-Not a bone of His body would be broken.

Psalm 35v11-He would be accused by false witnesses.

Psalm 41v9- A friend would betray Him.

Psalm 69v21-He would be given vinegar to drink.

Isaiah 50v6 – He would be scourged.

Isaiah 53v7-He would be silent before his accusers.

Zechariah 11v12- He would be sold for 30 pieces of silver.

We can say with certainty that the prophets of God were accurate and that God is faithful in every case by fulfilling His word through them. We know that God has shown us in His Feasts (His appointed times) what will take place and how Yeshua fulfils them. He has already fulfilled Passover, Unleavened Bread, First Fruits and the Feast of Weeks, known in Christendom as Pentecost.

We know that the Feast of Trumpets-Yom Teruah, Day of Atonement -Yom Kippur and Tabernacles- Sukkot has yet to be fulfilled by Yeshua and we can see how Yeshua, Paul and John in Revelation confirm the prophecies by Joel and Daniel and others regarding these Feasts.

We see that Ezekiel records his vision of the Millennial Temple and these Feasts continuing throughout the millennial reign of Yeshua. Take a look at Ezekiel 45 v 18-20 to see the Biblical New Year, Ezekiel 45 v 21-24 to see that Passover and Unleavened Bread are celebrated, Ezekiel 45 v 25 and Zechariah 14 v 16-21 to read of the celebration of Tabernacles.

If we can say with certainty that the word of God through the prophets have been fulfilled to date, then we must be able to say that prophecies regarding the future must also be fully relied on and trusted.

There is another point I want to make about Scripture and that is that God does not leave us guessing about what will take place. We may not see it but if we search hard enough in His word the answer is there.

For instance, it would have been hard for those living at the time of Yeshua to have connected Him to the Feast of Passover, the Exodus, Abraham's journey with Isaac to the mountain to sacrifice him, the red heifer sacrifice and much more, but it is all there in scripture. We just have to look at, study and in some cases be shown. That is why Paul wrote to the Gentiles, who didn't know scripture, to explain things to them.

When John wrote the book of Revelation he was in the Spirit realm looking into the return of the Messiah and His reign. He describes in detail what is to come and as we read his account of what he saw we see that he is describing the fulfilment of what many prophets, particularly Daniel, wrote. We must therefore rely on John's book as a confirmation of prophecy and look at the whole scripture to provide us with an explanation of those things which we find hard to understand. If we connect those prophecies which John uses with history we begin to get a picture of what the warning is about.

I have been examining the prophecies and connected history for some years now and have realised that much of what is being taught in Christendom, particularly about John's warning in Chapter 13 of the book of Revelation and the account of Yeshua's return by Paul in Chapter 4 of 1 Thessalonians and Chapter 2 of his second letter to the Thessalonians is not accurate, and leads us to believe things which are just not true. The danger of not understanding what John is saying is that we expect something which is not going to happen in the way we think, therefore we act accordingly and we are ill-prepared.

When I realised, after all my research, what the Mark of the Beast was which John wrote about in chapter thirteen of his book, I told my children exactly what I had found in an effort to prepare them properly for what is to come. I then taught my congregation.

We should all have a chance to evaluate scripture and its connected history and make up our own minds. This is why I wrote this small book to give you a chance to examine the facts and make up your own mind based on the prophecies and how they have and will be fulfilled.

If you agree the outworking for you will be life changing but it will be full of blessing and peace, which is why God gives us prophecy in the first place. Knowing that He is in control and we can trust Him and His Word; *"The Lord is faithful in all His words and gracious in all His deeds"* ~ Psalm 145 verse 13.

Chapter 1: John's warning - our future

We hear so much about the 'Mark of the Beast', the mark which is mentioned in Revelation 13. We use our imagination trying to understand what this peculiar mark is which John the writer of Revelation does not expound upon in this Chapter.

Could it be a computer chip like those we use on our dogs to identify them or could it be an identification card like the new passports? There is so much speculation and guess work and many within Christendom are left without a scriptural explanation by their leaders. We are left to wonder and in some cases told that it is not important as Yeshua is coming back so soon that it won't concern us.

A number of pastors have told me that we shouldn't teach on the book of Revelation and the book of Daniel because they are too hard to understand, therefore are not for our time. When John wrote the book of Revelation showing us the fulfilment of the Prophets centuries before did he do so believing that the Churches he wrote to earlier in his book would be left wondering about what the Mark was, and if so why are we left to wonder?

OR -are we really left to wonder? Or is John's lack of explanation because he assumed that the reader would understand the prophets, be a follower of Yeshua, the true Messiah and they would also know the scriptures which give a full explanation of the 'Mark on the forehead and right hand'.

I believe that John expected his readers to understand and that's why he wrote "This calls for Wisdom", v 18. Wisdom, as I will explain later, is not that only those who are clever will know, he is referring to those who know the Scriptures and follow the word of God, the Torah and the Prophets, which make up a large part of the

Tanach (Hebrew Scriptures/ 'Old Testament'). They will understand. Sadly many of us have not been taught from what is sadly called the Old Testament so we find it hard to understand. However my prayer is that through this study we will gain wisdom or at least begin to gain wisdom.

Let us first go to the verses in Revelation 13 in which John makes this statement. I am using the New Revised Standard Version for this scripture:

1 And I saw a beast rising out of the sea, having ten horns and seven heads; and on its horns were ten diadems, and on its heads were blasphemous names.

2 And the beast that I saw was like a leopard, its feet were like a bear's, and its mouth was like a lion's mouth. And the dragon gave it his power and his throne and great authority. 3 One of its heads seemed to have received a death-blow, but its mortal wound had been healed. In amazement the whole earth followed the beast.

4 They worshiped the dragon, for he had given his authority to the beast, and they worshiped the beast, saying, "Who is like the beast, and who can fight against it?"

5 The beast was given a mouth uttering haughty and blasphemous words, and it was allowed to exercise authority for forty-two months. 6 It opened its mouth to utter blasphemies against God, blaspheming his name and his dwelling, that is, those who dwell in heaven. 7 Also it was allowed to make war on the saints and to conquer them. It was given authority over every tribe and people and language and nation,

8 and all the inhabitants of the earth will worship it, everyone whose name has not been written from the foundation of the world in the book of life of the Lamb that was slaughtered. 9 Let anyone who has an ear listen:

[10] *If you are to be taken captive, into captivity you go; if you kill with the sword, with the sword you must be killed. Here is a call for the endurance and faith of the saints.*

[11] *Then I saw another beast that rose out of the earth; it had two horns like a lamb and it spoke like a dragon.*

[12] *It exercises all the authority of the first beast on its behalf, and it makes the earth and its inhabitants worship the first beast, whose mortal wound had been healed.*

[13] *It performs great signs, even making fire come down from heaven to earth in the sight of all;*

[14] *and by the signs that it is allowed to perform on behalf of the beast, it deceives the inhabitants of earth, telling them to make an image for the beast that had been wounded by the sword and yet lived;*

[15] *and it was allowed to give breath to the image of the beast so that the image of the beast could even speak and cause those who would not worship the image of the beast to be killed.*

[16] *Also it causes all, both small and great, both rich and poor, both free and slave, to be marked on the right hand or the forehead,*

[17] *so that no one can buy or sell who does not have the mark, that is, the name of the beast or the number of its name.*

[18] *This calls for wisdom: let anyone with understanding calculate the number of the beast, for it is the number of a person. Its number is six hundred sixty-six.*

John warned us a second time about false worship in the end times when he wrote in Rev 14:9-12 (ANIV):

[9]
A third angel followed them and said in a loud voice: "If anyone worships the beast and his image and receives his mark on the forehead or on the hand,

7

10

he, too, will drink of the wine of God's fury, which has been poured full strength into the cup of his wrath. He will be tormented with burning sulphur in the presence of the holy angels and of the Lamb.

11

And the smoke of their torment rises for ever and ever. There is no rest day or night for those who worship the beast and his image, or for anyone who receives the mark of his name."

12

This calls for patient endurance on the part of the saints who obey God's commandments and remain faithful to Jesus.

We can see that these events are certainly for a time in the future. They are events which will occur on the earth before the return of the Messiah. They concern a False Prophet described by John as the first beast who is to come and who will deceive the inhabitants of the earth and the second beast will cause them to worship a false image of the first beast and to receive a 'Mark' or the name of the beast or the number of his name.

The first Beast who is referred to here is the 'False Messiah' who is often wrongly described in Christendom as the Anti-Christ. This first beast comes out of the sea, meaning the peoples or nations, therefore he is a man.

The word antichrist gives us a picture of a person with satanic features, wearing black and performing satanic rituals and practices to control the masses. That will not be the case - he will come as saviour of the people, a man who will be looked upon as the true Messiah.

We read he is killed at one point and is resurrected. As a result the whole earth (except the wise) will worship him. He is given authority by the second beast, Satan himself, who is given power by God Himself to ensure that prophecy is fulfilled.

The words used by Yeshua to describe the first beast are the false Messiah, someone who calls himself a Messiah but is not. Yeshua says there will be many but in the end one will come who will convince the whole earth. The false Messiah will obviously be of Jewish background coming to save Jews and releasing them to carry out God's commands freely in The Land of Israel.

No one –Jew or Gentile would think of a Messiah of Israel as anyone other than Jewish. However this person does not encourage people to keep the commands of God by following the Torah and in fact encourages them to break the covenant of God with the Jewish people;

Daniel 11:32 (NRSV) *"He shall seduce with intrigue those who violate the covenant";*

For three and a half years, according to the Prophet Daniel, that happens. So to all intents and purposes he appears as a Messiah coming to save Israel and support those who keep God's commands.

After three and half years he is mortally wounded and resurrected according to John in Revelation 13. From that point we see that he turns against the Jewish people and the followers of the true Messiah-Yeshua.

Paul describes him as the lawless or correctly translated Torah-less one. This is what Paul says about him in 2 Thessalonians 2:1-4 ;

[1] As to the coming of our Lord Jesus Christ and our being gathered together to him, we beg you, brothers and sisters,

[2] not to be quickly shaken in mind or alarmed, either by spirit or by word or by letter, as though from us, to the effect that the day of the Lord is already here.

[3] Let no one deceive you in any way; for that day will not come unless the rebellion comes first and the lawless one is revealed, the one destined for destruction.

[4] He opposes and exalts himself above every so-called god or object of worship, so that he takes his seat in the temple of God,

9

declaring himself to be God.

So back to the 'Mark'- John tells us that it will be on their right hand or their forehead. As we will see the phrase 'on the forehead and right hand' is common in Scripture and interestingly John states that those with wisdom will understand this.

The book of Daniel Chapter 12 v 10 says that in these times, meaning the times of the False Messiah, *"None of the wicked will understand, but those who are wise will understand".* Let's go to the next point then to understand the wise.

Chapter 2: Who are the wise?

According to many scriptures the wise are those who understand and have knowledge of the Torah-The Laws of God. We have to look at scripture to understand who is considered wise, as scripture determined the thinking and understanding of those living at the time John wrote in the first century.

These were Jews in the diaspora and Gentiles who had joined them in their belief that Yeshua was the Messiah and had fulfilled the Torah and the Prophets. So he wrote to seven "Churches", or synagogues, as it should have been translated, who were all on the same page in their understanding of the Messiah and with the terminology of the scriptures.

What therefore does scripture say about wisdom or the wise?

"See, I have taught you decrees and laws as the LORD my God commanded me, so that you may follow them in the land you are entering to take possession of it. ⁶ Observe them carefully, for this will show your wisdom and understanding to the nations, who will hear about all these decrees and say, "Surely this great nation is a wise and understanding people." Deuteronomy 4:5-6 (ANIV)

The law of the LORD is perfect, reviving the soul. The statutes of the LORD are trustworthy, making wise the simple. Psalms 19:7 (ANIV)

"The fear of the LORD is the beginning of wisdom; all who follow his precepts have good understanding. To him belongs eternal praise." Psalms 111:10 (ANIV)

"Get wisdom, get understanding; do not forget my words or swerve from them. ⁶ Do not forsake wisdom, and she will protect

you; love her, and she will watch over you." Proverbs 4:5-6 (ANIV*)*

"Having in the Law the embodiment of knowledge and of the truth" Romans 2:20 *(*NASB77)

There are many other scriptures referring to the wise understanding the Torah, but this one refers to the Messiah Yeshua (Jesus) having that understanding and wisdom.

"A shoot will come up from the stump of Jesse; from his roots a Branch will bear fruit. [2] The Spirit of the LORD will rest on him-the Spirit of wisdom and of understanding, the Spirit of counsel and of power, the Spirit of knowledge and of the fear of the LORD- [3] and he will delight in the fear of the LORD." Isaiah 11:1-3 *(*ANIV)

Should we therefore ask the Lord to teach us the knowledge we need?

"Teach me knowledge and good judgment, for I believe in your commands. [67] Before I was afflicted I went astray, but now I obey your word. [68] You are good, and what you do is good; teach me your decrees." Psalms 119:66-68 (ANIV)

"Do good to your servant according to your word, O LORD. [66] Teach me knowledge and good judgment, for I believe in your commands." Psalms 119:65-66 *(*ANIV)

"Teach me knowledge and good judgment, for I believe in your commands. [67] Before I was afflicted I went astray, but now I obey your word. [68] You are good, and what you do is good; teach me your decrees." Psalms 119:66-68 *(*ANIV)

What about those who don't have such wisdom;

*"My people are destroyed from lack of knowledge. Because you have rejected knowledge, I also reject you as my priests; because you have ignored the law of your God, "*Hosea 4:6 (ANIV)

"Not everyone who says to Me, 'Lord, Lord,' shall enter the

kingdom of heaven, but he who does the will of My Father in heaven. 22 Many will say to Me in that day, 'Lord, Lord, have we not prophesied in Your name, cast out demons in Your name, and done many wonders in Your name?' 23 And then I will declare to them, 'I never knew you; depart from Me, you who practice lawlessness! (without Torah) "Matt 7:21-23 (NKJV)

Yeshua is quoting from Psalm 119 - verse 115 where the Psalmist tells those who do not keep Torah *"Go away from me, you evildoers, that I may keep the commandments of my God".*

I have not used all the scriptures which enforce the concept that those who understand the Torah (the Laws of God) are those who are wise and understanding, as there are many. I will also elaborate further in regard to the wise and foolish virgins when answering a question posed by a friend regarding salvation.

However I think it is clear that these scriptures point to the people who John is talking about when he says that they will be able to work out the number and have understanding of his message. I think I have also been able to demonstrate from scripture that those who have knowledge of God's Laws and practice them are those who are considered wise.

This makes a great deal of sense to me as many, like myself, are not academics but love God and His word with all our hearts. Paul refers to people who love God and His word when he writes Romans Chapter 2 v 13 to 15

"I am passionate about God's instructions and I know He has written them on my heart".

One further point I want to make here is that those in first century Judea who are referred to as walking in the light are those keeping Torah and those in darkness ignoring it.

The next thing we need to do is to examine the elements in this passage which involve the Mark.

Chapter 3: Two systems of worship

There are four main elements concerning the Mark and the first to deal with is the element of worship. Worship is the key to all that John is saying.

John makes it very clear to us in verse 12 of Revelation Chapter 13 that Satan's goal is to have us worship the first beast and his image. We must understand from this statement about worship that this is not about a political system or Governmental system; it is about a worship system.

Hang on to that point please because there are many saying that this political person or that King is the false Messiah. Satan is trying to have them worship anything other than God Himself. He is not concerned about politics or Kings and Queens; he is focused on pulling us away from worshipping God almighty-The Holy One of Israel.

We see throughout all of scripture, even from the beginning, from the time in the Garden, God has been speaking to us about relationship with Him, the Almighty Creator of both the Heavens and the Earth. We read of God speaking to Noah about the world which had rejected Him. When He called Abraham it was a call for Abraham to follow God and His ways, and that's why in James Chapter 2 v 23 God calls Abraham His friend.

Abraham had a choice to remain with his family and continue to follow the gods of his fathers and ignore the Laws of God. Abraham didn't follow the practices of his family and community in their pagan worship with all its laws and calendars of worship, but he chose to follow God's Laws and commandments. Genesis 26 v 5.

God laws are specific regulations for the people of Israel to follow and they have specific times allotted to them by God. They are laws which enable a deeper and fuller relationship with God based on covenant. These laws we refer to are better translated "Divine Regulations" and are known as the "Torah" (the first five books of the Bible) or are referred to now in most biblical translations as the Law.

They include all the commandments of God which help us not to fall into sin. Paul wrote:

"Therefore no-one will be declared righteous in his sight by observing the law; rather, through the law we become conscious of sin." Romans 3:20 (ANIV)

The outworking of this relationship with God is worship, not only in the form of a congregation meeting once or twice a week, but in a complete lifestyle which God has set out in scripture. This is why Yeshua and Paul teach throughout their ministry that we should follow Torah rather than the traditions of man. Why? Because man-made practices are often opposite to the ways of God and lead us into false worship and at times other than those appointed by God. These are just some of the Scriptures which help us to understand this.

"Why do you also transgress the commandment of God because of your tradition?" Matt 15:3 (NKJV)

"Thus you nullify the word of God by your tradition that you have handed down. And you do many things like that." Mark 7:13 (ANIV)

"See to it that no-one takes you captive through hollow and deceptive philosophy, which depends on human tradition and the basic principles of this world rather than on Christ." Col 2:8 (ANIV)

Jacob, re-named James when the King James Bible was translated from the Geneva Bible to please the King, makes it clear that there is only one Law- giver and that is God.

"Brothers, do not slander one another. Anyone who speaks against his brother or judges him speaks against the law and judges it. When you judge the law, you are not keeping it, but sitting in judgment on it. [12] *There is only one Lawgiver and Judge, the one who is able to save and destroy. But you—who are you to judge your neighbour?" Jacob (James)* 4:11-12 (ANIV)

I want to repeat what I said earlier about what Yeshua told those who minister in his name - to go away from Him. Why? It is because they ministered without the Torah. The English Standard version best translates this passage; Matthew 7:21-23 (ESV)

[21] *"Not everyone who says to me, 'Lord, Lord,' will enter the kingdom of heaven, but the one who does the will of my Father who is in heaven.* [22] *On that day many will say to me, 'Lord, Lord, did we not prophesy in your name, and cast out demons in your name, and do many mighty works in your name?'* [23] *And then will I declare to them, 'I never knew you; depart from me, you workers of lawlessness.'*

So is there another Law giver or be it a false lawgiver? Yes there is-Satan himself, who we see changes the times, seasons and Laws.

"He shall speak pompous words against the Most High, Shall persecute the saints of the Most High, and shall intend to change times and law." Dan 7:25 (NKJV)

Satan's laws dictate a system of worship along with a calendar of worship which are contrary to that which God sets out in The Torah.

We will see that the Laws of God or the laws of Satan involve worship systems - practices and commands which are a system involving times and seasons, one being in line with God and one in line with Satan. To coin a phrase, "never the twain shall meet", because what has light to do with darkness?

"If we claim to have fellowship with him yet walk in the darkness, we lie and do not live by the truth." 1 John 1:6 (ANIV)

"What harmony is there between Christ and Belial?" 2 Corinthians 6:15 (ANIV)

Belial is sin, falsehood and false worship. Satan has clearly changed these Laws of God as we will see as we read on.

God's worship system or Calendar for worship is set out in Leviticus 23 and as we will read in the following scriptures its purpose is to separate worship of Him from any connection to pagan worship. This is because the calendar of worship to God points to the Messiah who fulfils the Torah.

The following scripture is made clear when we understand that the Hebrews have been living in Egypt for 430 years. They are brought out into the wilderness with all the baggage of slavery but also all the baggage of living in a pagan community which worshiped their leaders, their animal kingdom and the natural kingdom such as the sun and stars. They worshipped with symbolism on specific times and dates.

The Hebrews are about to enter Canaanite country which has a similar system to that of the Egyptians, and God says this to the Israelites;

"You shall not do as they do in the land of Egypt, where you lived, and you shall not do as they do in the land of Canaan, to which I am bringing you. You shall not walk in their statutes. [4] You shall follow my rules and keep my statutes and walk in them. I am the LORD your God. [5] You shall therefore keep my statutes and my rules; if a person does them, he shall live by them: I am the LORD." Lev 18:3-5 (ESV)

God also knows that a mixture of worship or patterns of worship is a sign that mankind is not fully committed to Him and His word. He knows that once we involve pagan elements in our worship we move away from Him. God pleads with Israel not to get involved with this false worship or false practices in any way, shape or form because we are as easily deceived as Adam and Eve were in the garden.

"When the LORD your God cuts off before you the nations whom you go in to dispossess, and you dispossess them and dwell in their land, [30] take care that you be not ensnared to follow them, after they have been destroyed before you, and that you do not inquire about their gods, saying, 'How did these nations serve their gods?—that I also may do the same.' [31] You shall not worship the LORD your God in that way." Deuteronomy 12:29-31 (ESV)

How then are these worship systems expressed? We see from Scripture that God gives specific instructions as to when, times and dates, people are to gather together to worship and how to worship. Also He gives a specific time when we should, as He did in creation, rest from our labours.

These are most clearly seen in Leviticus 23. I will ask you to read that yourself and in doing so you will see that God gives specific times, dates and seasons to rest and to celebrate, which He makes very clear are His appointed times and are His Festivals, not Israel's or the Church's - but His.

You will see He is specific about the times, for example the day of rest on the seventh day, as He did when He created the earth. He gives specific times for the Festivals such as Passover which He decrees will be on the 14th day of the first month. All these Festivals you will see have specific timings and all point to the Messiah –Yeshua, and that is why Yeshua says;

"Do not think that I came to destroy the Law or the Prophets. I did not come to destroy but to fulfil. [18] For assuredly, I say to you, till heaven and earth pass away, one jot or one tittle will by no means pass from the law till all is fulfilled." Matt 5:17-18 (NKJV)

Not all of these Festivals are yet fulfilled. He has fulfilled Passover, Unleavened Bread, First Fruits and Feast of Weeks. However we are looking forward to Him fulfilling the Feast of

Trumpets, The Day of Atonement and the Festival of Tabernacles when He will dwell on earth again.

These are God's system of worship which is Prophetic and Messianic, giving us a picture of God's desire that salvation shall come to all who believe and repent. All of these were in place before the foundation of the earth.

We see clearly from the Book of Genesis Chapter 1 v 14 that God placed the stars, Sun and moon to be signs for the seasons and days.

In the One New Man Bible it is translated to be signs for the:

'Appointed Times'.

In the Holman Christian Standard Bible it is translated:

Then God said, "Let there be lights in the expanse of the sky to separate the day from the night. They will serve as signs for festivals and for days and years".

In the NRSV it translates:

"And God said, "Let there be lights in the dome of the sky to separate the day from the night; and let them be for signs and for seasons and for days and years".

We can see therefore that the appointed times/Festivals which all speak about the Messiah were in place before the creation of the World, such is the importance of celebrating Sabbath and the Feasts of the Lord. Strong's Concordance shows us that the word sign in this verse means "Divine Communication".

When we celebrate the Lord's Appointed Times we are in direct communication with the creator of the universe. All I can say about that is - it is nothing less than amazing. When we look at the importance of the Torah in this way would Yeshua or Paul change the Torah? Certainly not!

The Apostle John tells us:

"In the beginning was the Word, and the Word was with God, and the Word was God." John 1:1 (ANIV)

"In Him was life, and that life was the light of men." John 1:3-4 (ANIV)

"The Word became flesh and made his dwelling among us." John 1:14 (ANIV)

"The beast that you saw was, and is not, and is about to rise from the bottomless pit and go to destruction. And the dwellers on earth, whose names have not been written in the book of life from the foundation of the world... "Rev 17:8 (ESV)

The Living Word of God is revealed in the whole of Scripture including Torah, and was in existence before He created the world. Genesis 1 v 14 says this in Holman's Christian Standard Bible, which is closest to the meaning of this particular scripture:

Genesis 1:14 (HCSB):

[14] Then God said, "Let there be lights in the expanse of the sky to separate the day from the night. They will serve as signs for Festivals and for days and years".

The word sign here in the original reads "a supernatural event" meaning a Divine Communication (Strong's no. 253).

This clearly shows us that the Stars, Moon and Sun were placed in the sky to provide us with the timing of the Festivals - God's 'Appointed Times' as referred to in Leviticus 23 and which all point to the Messiah. I think we would all agree that this is amazing but also really important to us to understand because they show us the correct timing for the calendar of worship as set out in Leviticus 23.

This means that through these Festivals and the calendar of worship which God gives us, the timing of which is designated by

God Himself, we are shown that any other timing for worship is false. For example Christmas (25th December) is not the Festival at which God shows us He dwells with man. The Festival which fulfils this is Tabernacles which falls in the autumn. It is clear that Yeshua was born at this time, thereby fulfilling Tabernacles (the complete fulfilment is on His return).

He was certainly not born on 25th December. This date was the date for the celebration of the birth of Mithra the sun god whose symbol is the evergreen tree. Christmas with all its paraphernalia is the 1st - 6th century Roman feast called Saturnalia celebrating Mithra.

When we examine Gods Feasts and the Prophets, all pointing to the Messiah, we can better understand what John is saying to us because Yeshua is the fulfilment of those prophetic writings put in place in the spirit realm by God outside of our time as we understand it. We see in the book of Hebrews that all the things which take place within the Torah are also taking place in Heaven;

"For if He (Yeshua) were on earth, He would not be a priest, since there are priests who offer the gifts according to the law; ^{5} who serve the copy and shadow of the heavenly things, as Moses was divinely instructed when he was about to make the tabernacle." Hebrews 8:4-5 (NKJV)

Reading from Genesis chapter three we see that the woman saw that the tree was to be desired to make one wise;

"So when the woman saw that the tree was good for food, that it was pleasant to the eyes, and a tree desirable to make one wise ..." Gen 3:6 (NKJV).

Genesis Chapter 3 verse 7 says their eyes were opened and from that point man and woman became aware of sin, because as we have read Paul makes it clear that the Torah- the Laws of God-makes us aware of sin.

The tree therefore is connected to the Divine regulations which

God gives us as a pattern for living and worship.

Once man gained this knowledge Satan was in a position to draw him away to his pattern or system, and from that time on man chose for himself which he would follow. There is an interesting phenomenon here because when we look at worship of Satan it comes in the form of worship of many gods which man has created but we are actually created by God Himself to worship Him.

Man has always struggled with this because of the forces of the spirit of the air - Satan who would have us believe that our ways are better than God's. That is why we see in Christendom so much tradition based on our own desire to create our own pattern or practice of worship, rather than following the one God created for us.

That is why Yeshua said:

"You have a fine way of setting aside the commands of God in order to observe your own traditions" Mark 7:9 (ANIV)

"Why do you also transgress the commandment of God because of your tradition?" Matt 15:3 (NKJV)

"Thus you nullify the word of God by your tradition that you have handed down. And you do many things like that." Mark 7:13 (ANIV)

Paul adds to this by saying;

"See to it that no-one takes you captive through hollow and deceptive philosophy, which depends on human tradition and the basic principles of this world rather than on Christ". Col 2:8 *(ANIV)*

Paul also goes on to stress that we should not let go of God's Laws, the Torah, because of our faith that we are saved by Grace, because he knows that Satan is at work trying to ensnare us to make us follow a false pattern of worship:

"For the mystery of lawlessness (Torah-lessness) is already at work"

2 Thessalonians 2:7 (NKJV):

"What shall we say then? Shall we continue in sin that grace may abound? 2 Certainly not!"

Romans 6:1-2 (NKJV):

"Do we then make void the law (Torah) through faith? Certainly not! On the contrary, we establish the law." Romans 3:31 (NKJV)

Paul then warns us about the time when mankind follows his own ways, believing what is false because they do not know the truth, being Gods patterns of worship and Yeshua fulfilling them:

"The coming of the lawless one is according to the working of Satan, with all power, signs, and lying wonders, [10] and with all unrighteous deception among those who perish, because they did not receive the love of the truth, that they might be saved.[11] And for this reason God will send them strong delusion, that they should believe the lie, [12] that they all may be condemned who did not believe the truth but had pleasure in unrighteousness." 2 Thessalonians 2:9-12 (NKJV)

The word lawlessness, placed in its proper context, means Torah-lessness. Paul is at pains to tell the Jewish believers in Rome to abide by the Torah as an example to the Gentile believers. He doesn't want the Gentiles to accuse them of not glorifying God, and in so doing allowing the Gentile believers to stray also;

"You who make your boast in the law, do you dishonour God through breaking the law? 24 For 'the name of God is blasphemed among the Gentiles because of you,'" Romans 2:23-24 (NKJV)

We must not forget that the Torah continues in the future through the Millennial reign of Yeshua, enforced by Him through the nation of Israel who are filled with His Spirit and keep Torah;

"I will give you (Jews) a new heart and put a new spirit within you; I will take the heart of stone out of your flesh and give you a heart of flesh.[27] I will put My Spirit within you and cause you to walk in My statutes, and you will keep My judgments and do them." Ezekiel 36:26-27 (NKJV)

As I stated in the foreword, in Ezekiel 45 we read that the Festivals from Passover to Tabernacles are celebrated in the Millennial Temple, as are many offerings, and in Zechariah 14 we see that there is punishment for those who don't celebrate the Feast of Tabernacles. All these scriptures lead us to understand that the Festivals –the calendar of worship - are celebrated throughout the millennial reign of Yeshua. Throughout this time all the nations which are left after the Judgement of the Nations in Mathew 25 will receive the Torah from Jerusalem;

"For out of Zion shall go forth the law, and the word of the LORD *from Jerusalem."* Micah 4:2 (ESV)

When we look at Abraham we see that he was called to establish true worship and blessing through his offspring, the Jews. The nations would be blessed because Abraham obeyed God's voice and kept God's laws even before God gave them to Moses:

"I will give to your descendants all these lands; and in your seed all the nations of the earth shall be blessed; [5] because Abraham obeyed My voice and kept My charge, My commandments, My statutes, and My laws." Gen 26:4-5 (NKJV)

That is why the Jews were given the manual (Bible) for the calendar and system of worship and because of this they are the focus of Satan's hate. If he, Satan, can destroy the messenger then the world will be unable to identify the true Messiah and his False Messiah will go unchallenged by men.

However, in Daniel 11 we read the story about the reign of the False Messiah, and in that chapter we read that there will be those who teach the covenant of God and His Laws to the many. This is because Satan cannot destroy them and these are the ones I spoke about earlier who are wise and understand;

"And those of the people who understand shall instruct many;"
Dan 11:33 (NKJV)

I am certain that I will be accused by those who are keeping the
traditions of man that I am teaching a doctrine of being saved only
by the Torah and not by the grace of God through the blood of His
Son who cleanses us of all sin. I can answer this by referring those
critics to the scriptures I have already mentioned.

There are many other scriptures that I have not mentioned in
support of our need to keep to Gods patterns of worship. I cannot
find one scripture to support anything about changing God's
calendar of worship. What about grace? Well, grace cannot be
valid without there being the Laws of God.

We are saved from the consequences of breaking The Law because
of grace. It is because of the love of God for us that He gives us
grace, because without it we would face eternal death. So we are
saved by the grace of God given as an act of love.

We should, therefore, show our love by keeping His laws, His
decrees and His statutes, not those of man and ultimately the laws
of Satan himself. To obtain that grace, however, we have to believe
that Yeshua is Messiah and repent of our sins as defined by Torah.

Yeshua says this:

*"Whoever has my commands and obeys them, he is the one who
loves me. He who loves me will be loved by my Father, and I too
will love him and show myself to him."* John 14:21.

We must also understand that repentance is turning away from
false worship and a false lifestyle which God, by giving us His
Torah, tries to prevent us from practising.

Satan does everything possible to have us practice false worship
enabling us to follow him. He deceives us into keeping the
traditions of man; he ensnares us into moving away from Gods

patterns into his own patterns of worship. He deceives us into practicing non-biblical patterns of worship such as Christmas, Easter and Sunday which are patterns of false worship as I will show you later. He has us ignore truth because of fear of man and has us worship blindly because he has led us to believe that our religious leaders know all things and therefore must be followed.

The established churches have used these principles to deceive millions of sincere believers. We are conditioned to believe in certain ways ánd practice our faith in certain ways in order that, when the time comes, we are conditioned to worship the image of the Beast as described by John in Revelation 13. Satan will use anything to deceive us.

A born again evangelical friend asked this question;

Question: *Up till now I can fully understand what you have written. Read some eye-opening stuff too! But about this last bit. Usually in our evangelical circles we hear about sin being a lot of bad things that we need to turn away from. The focus is always on sins like unbelief, selfishness, greed and so on (and rightly so, isn't it) – but never about which days or feasts we keep. I think for most of us, these things are never questioned.*

This is what comes to my mind here, while reading. I mean: would you say that even born-again Christians, sincerely living in relationship with the Lord, would in the end times be subjected to worshiping the enemy, and as a result... even be lost? That's the impression I get here. I find that really puzzling. Could you address that?

Thank you for a great question! First of all I want to point out that my answers are actually what Yeshua, Paul and John make clear to us in Scripture. They are not my own opinions. I want to answer you with their words and this is what they say.

Paul makes it clear that the Torah, which includes a pattern of worship set out in Leviticus 23 and in many other scriptures, defines sin. He writes this in Romans chapter 7 v 7.

"What then should we say? That the law is sin? By no means! Yet, if it had not been for the law, I would not have known sin".

We have to know the Torah to define sin or we have to have the Torah on our hearts to know what sin is by way of conviction.

God makes it so clear that we should celebrate seven Festivals all of which point to Him. They have specific times and are in line with specific seasons. If we look clearly at these Festivals Yeshua fulfils each one as He explains in Matthew Chapter 5 v 17. These Festivals do not in any way focus on any other worship practice.

So by knowing and keeping the Festivals God gave us we are not drawn away from them into the sin of doing what the pagans do. Paul tells us in Romans Chapter 3 v 31 that we should *"uphold the Torah"*-The Laws of God. Why? Because they are our guide to true worship and anything outside of that is not true worship, it is sin.

Look at what God says about worshipping in the way of the nations in Deuteronomy 12 verses 30 and 31;

[30] and after they have been destroyed before you, be careful not to be ensnared by enquiring about their gods, saying, "How do these nations serve their gods? We will do the same." [31] You must not worship the LORD your God in their way, because in worshipping their gods, they do all kinds of detestable things the LORD hates".

In the following letter to the Thessalonians which you have read earlier Paul wrote that the spirit of Torah-lessness is already at work in his time and that a man of Lawlessness is to come. This is the False Messiah who will turn man away from God and His Laws. To a great extent that has already happened within Christendom and dates, times, seasons and laws which are not of God are in place in our worship system.

There are so many things which we do in Christendom which are not Biblical and may seem unimportant, but if they are outside the

Torah God must think they are important. At the end of time when the man of Lawlessness or Torah-lessness is revealed it will become clear that he opposes God in every way and yet there will be those who will say: 'does it matter that we don't keep the Laws of God? This man is God so we do as he says'.

My main point in answering my friend's question is answered by Yeshua Himself when in Matthew Chapter 7 v 21 - 23. Ministers will go before Yeshua at the end of time and proclaim they did many things in His name. Yeshua's response is clear as you read earlier. He says, 'Away from me, you did so without the Torah'. How much clearer can that be?

Then we read in Mathew 25 verses 1 to 13 the story Yeshua told in His discourse regarding His return that there were foolish and wise virgins. All believed but only 5 were taken to be with him and it was those who had oil in their lamps. I have described earlier what being wise means, it means keeping Torah. This is what we are told about those waiting for Him at the end of time;

[1] "Then the kingdom of heaven will be like this. Ten bridesmaids took their lamps and went to meet the bridegroom.

[2] Five of them were foolish, and five were wise.

[3] When the foolish took their lamps, they took no oil with them;

[4] but the wise took flasks of oil with their lamps.

[5] As the bridegroom was delayed, all of them became drowsy and slept.

[6] But at midnight there was a shout, 'Look! Here is the bridegroom! Come out to meet him.'

[7] Then all those bridesmaids got up and trimmed their lamps.

[8] The foolish said to the wise, 'Give us some of your oil, for our lamps are going out.'

^{9} *But the wise replied, 'No! there will not be enough for you and for us; you had better go to the dealers and buy some for yourselves.'*

^{10} *And while they went to buy it, the bridegroom came, and those who were ready went with him into the wedding banquet; and the door was shut.*

^{11} *Later the other bridesmaids came also, saying, 'Lord, lord, open to us.'*

^{12} *But he replied, 'Truly I tell you, I do not know you.'*

^{13} *Keep awake therefore, for you know neither the day nor the hour.*

This parable is one of a number of parables running through Matthew Chapter 24 and into Chapter 25. The parables are about doing the will of God and obeying Him. In verses 11-13 of Matthew Chapter 24 Yeshua says;

^{11} *And many false prophets will arise and lead many astray.*

^{12} *And because of the increase of lawlessness, the love of many will grow cold.*

^{13} *But the one who endures to the end will be saved.*

First of all we can see that Yeshua is speaking about the False Messiah and Lawlessness (Torah-lessness) prior to the parable of the ten virgins.

In first century Judea when Yeshua was speaking these words the meaning of being foolish were for those who did not keep the Torah. I know many teach that Yeshua was speaking about The Holy Spirit who is also connected in scripture to oil however we have to look at the meaning of the lamps they were holding.

Five didn't have oil in them so they couldn't burn and shine a light and shining a light is very important. Why? It is because, in first century Judea, a lamp was a symbol of a light for the Torah. So what Yeshua said was and is today obviously very important. However the understanding must come from scripture to be valid so let me explain.

Let me take you back to what I said about Genesis 1v14 and God putting lights in the sky as lights for the Festivals. Isaiah 42 verse 6 makes it clear that Israel are called to be righteous and to be a light to the Nations;

"I am the LORD, I have called you in righteousness, I have taken you by the hand and kept you; I have given you as a covenant to the people, a light to the nations".

Righteousness and covenant speak of the Torah. Isaiah is a prophet to comfort Israel but also to speak about the Messiah so the 'Light' here is the Messiah.

Who is the 'Light'? In John 8 v 12 Yeshua said:

"I am the Light of the world".

John 9 v 5 reads that Yeshua said

"I am The Light of the world".

In John 12 v 46 Yeshua says

"I have come as Light into the world"

...The purpose being that we should not remain in darkness. John 1 v 1-4 explains in full, connecting Yeshua the Word of God, the living Torah, to Yeshua being the Light who brings life;

[1] In the beginning was the Word, and the Word was with God, and the Word was God. [2] He was in the beginning with God. [3] All things came into being through him, and without him not one thing came into being. What has come into being [4] in him was life, and the life was the light of all people.

'In the beginning' ---Do we now see what John is saying? ... The worship system and the Torah which sets it in place were there before the lights in the sky which connects to our understanding from Genesis 1v14 as we read earlier.

Those hearing Yeshua would have been very familiar with Psalm 119 which is all about the Torah-The Laws of God-The Word of God. This is what we read in a verse many of us know so well; Psalm 119 v 105

"Your word is a lamp to my feet and a light to my path".

Proverbs 6 v 23 states:

"For the commandment is a lamp and the teaching a light, and the reproofs of discipline are the way of life"

Proverbs 13 verse 9 states;

"The light of the righteous rejoices, but the lamp of the wicked goes out".

What about the oil? Well, oil in scripture is precious and the wise seek it as we see in Proverbs 21 v 20;

"There is desirable treasure, and oil in the dwelling of the wise, But a foolish man squanders it".

God gives us oil- Torah- to make us shine His Light;

Psalm 104:15:

"And wine that makes glad the heart of man, Oil to make his face shine, and bread which strengthens man's heart".

I think I have made it clear what the understanding was in first century Judea. I am sure all those who heard Yeshua understood what He was saying in those times. However today, with the false teaching that Yeshua and Paul taught against the Torah, most of us don't understand and are thrown by unscriptural explanations.

This is why I say that I don't believe for one moment that God will judge harshly those who don't know about the things I am disclosing in this book.

 In finally answering my friend's question, if we sincerely believe what we have been taught about Torah and have no idea about the Feasts, God will not judge us for what we don't know and therefore our belief in Yeshua will take us to be with Him in eternity.

However, once one does know then that makes a difference and we are in rebellion. I hope that helps.

In Father's House, my congregation, we follow the Feasts as set out in Scripture and have enjoyed keeping the seventh day Sabbath and all the Feasts for many years now. We are trying to shine the Light of the Torah for others to follow; in other words, as in Daniel, we are trying to give understanding. I encourage you to do the same.

I hope this answers my friend's question.

Chapter 4: False worship

The relationship between Satan and man begins in the Garden of Eden. False worship becomes an issue for mankind after the expulsion from the garden.

When Yeshua spoke about Abel in Mathew 23 v 35 He called Abel righteous meaning He was obedient to the Torah. Now we know that the Tree of Knowledge of good and evil in the garden was the Torah. Clearly when Cain and Abel brought their offerings before God they were performing an act of worship which must have been defined by some divine instruction which can only be Torah.

When we look at the call God put upon Cain and Abel, we see that between them they could make offerings and sacrifices in accordance with Torah because Abel was a shepherd and could perform sacrifices for sin and Cain was a man of the soil so he could bring offerings of goodwill and thanks. However we read in Genesis 4 v 4-5 that Cain's offering was not accepted.

[4] and Abel for his part brought of the firstlings of his flock, their fat portions. And the LORD had regard for Abel and his offering, [5] but for Cain and his offering he had no regard. So Cain was very angry, and his countenance fell

Why then was Cain's offering not acceptable. There are many arguments about this but both men brought things which were valid in accordance with the Torah but clearly Cain's for some reason was invalid. To make an offering or sacrifice valid it has to be brought to the place designated at the right time.

There is no instruction as far as I can see about the place of the offering or sacrifice at that time although I do feel it would have been on Mount Moriah. But the lights in the sky gave Cain and Abel the timing. William J Morford in his translation of the Bible-The One New Man Bible, writes this about the reason for God rejecting Cain's offering;

"This actually refers to time, that Abel's offering was timely while Cain's was not"

Was it that Cain brought his offering at the wrong time? I can only agree wholeheartedly with Morford as timing for our worship of God is crucial in the spirit realm. God made the stars in the sky in order for us to know the timing of offerings and sacrifices and worshipping at any other time is false worship as Cain found to his cost.

This is why Yeshua called Abel righteous, meaning Torah keeping, showing us that Cain did not keep Torah.

Cain's actions were rebellion to God's Torah and man's rebellion continued until the flood when all those who sin are destroyed and all mankind is removed from the earth, with the exception of Noah, his family and their offspring.

Soon the descendants of Noah return to false worship and Nimrod the great grandson of Noah becomes the founder of a worship system which opposes God Himself. Nimrod is described in Genesis 10 v 9 as a mighty hunter, meaning he is opposed to God.

He establishes a tower of false worship in Babylon. As a result God scatters the people of Babylon. However Nimrod had established priesthood and a system of worship which continues to this day even within Christendom itself.

The Babylonian system of worship is seen in the book of Daniel in the description of the four Empires described as beasts in Daniel Chapter 7. We see first of all a lion representing Babylon, a bear representing the Medo-Persian Empire, a leopard representing Greece and a beast representing the fourth and final of man's Empires - Rome, which still operates today.

I know you are asking yourself, hasn't the Roman Empire been destroyed? You are correct in political/military terms but in spiritual terms it remains strong, because today the vast majority of churches in Christendom continue with a false system of worship which is established by Rome, but in actual fact is rooted in Babylon and includes the worship systems of all four empires. John refers to these religious Empires again at the beginning of Chapter 13 of the book of Revelation;

"Now the beast which I saw was like a leopard, his feet were like the feet of a bear, and his mouth like the mouth of a lion." Rev 13:2 (NKJV)

In Babylon the system of worship was related directly to sun worship; Baal was the Sun God of the East. In Babylon Baal was called Bel; Sunday was the solar weekly day of worship for all Bel worshippers. This was the "Venerable" day of the sun.

The winter solstice and the spring equinox were times of special celebrations and later became times of the birth of the sun god Mithra, which was established on 25th December and of the fertility goddess Eostre at the spring equinox, set to the same moon cycle as Easter is today.

This false worship system was established in Babylon with a priesthood and the Babylonian society was structured on this very system of worship. When the Medo-Persians conquered the Babylonian Empire in 537 BC the Babylonian priesthood led a community of pagan worshippers to safety in Pergamos, also known as Pergamum, which is situated in Turkey, 16 miles inland from the Aegean Sea.

John in Revelation 2 v 13 refers to Pergamum as the seat of Satan. The city became the site of the temple to Aesculapius, the Greek god of healing, and the seat of Babylonian sun worship, 'Mithraism', a centre of idolatry and of demon controlled religions with splendid temples. It attracted people from all over the Roman Empire to worship and seek healing in these pagan temples.

One of the temples was of 'Zeus the Saviour'. In 212 BC Pergamum, governed by Attalus 1st the Babylonian High Priest, made an alliance with Rome, becoming a voluntary member of the Empire and so coming under its protection. In turn, Rome aligned herself with the worship of its gods and absorbed many of the practices connected with this worship, culminating in 67 BC with the designation of Mithraism as the official state religion of the Roman Empire.

The island of Patmos, where John was living when he wrote down the revelation which God gave to him, is only a short distance from Pergamum. In John's time it had become the seat of satanic sun worship and John knew what was going on there.

Attalus 3rd, the Babylonian High Priest in Pergamum was known as the 'Pontiff', meaning 'bridge between natural and spiritual'. As he had no heir, he made a covenant with Rome that when he died he would leave Pergamum and the rights of the Babylonian priesthood to Rome. He died in 133 BC when the city and the spiritual authority of the priesthood, together with its religious practices, came under the authority and guardianship of the Roman emperors.

This responsibility as Babylonian Priest was passed on eventually to Emperor Constantine. During his reign he forced through changes to the Feasts, Festivals and Sabbath which both Jews and the early believers celebrated. I want to mention, and this is reiterated later, that whilst reigning as Babylonian Priest, Constantine moulded together Christianity, Mithraism and Isis (Eostre) worship by making the Mithra and Isis Feasts-Christmas, Easter and Sunday- the only Feast days to be celebrated in the Empire.

His focus and priority was the establishment of a calendar of worship based on the worship of the unconquerable sun-Mithra and the fertility goddess Eostre. The Babylonian Priesthood remained with the Roman Emperors until 376 AD when a Christian emperor called 'Gratian' refused to formalise the Babylonian covenant upon himself. This covenant was passed on to Damasus, the Bishop of Rome at that time. Damasus was renowned for his divisive and violent nature, and in 381 AD became the First Supreme Bishop of Rome, the Pontiff and Priest of the Babylonian covenant.

The name "Pontiff" means bridge between heaven and earth and was the name used for the Babylonian High Priest. Damasus introduced the worship of Mary/Child and endorsed the celebration of Easter, Sunday and Mithra-Christmas.

Damasus continued with the formal dress of the Pontiff (Babylonian Priest) so that the priesthood wore scarlet and purple, with a vest covered in pearls and a mitre adorned with gold and precious stones.

It was Damasus who ordered Jerome (who had called the Jews "Judaic serpents") to translate the Bible into Latin and Jerome was later canonised for this work. Edward Gibbon, the historian, in his book 'The Downfall of Rome' published in 1781, wrote about the Church in Rome at the time of Damasus (378 AD – 395 AD):

"In exact proportion as paganism has disappeared from without the church, in the very same proportion it appears in it. Pagan dresses for the priests, pagan festivals for the people, pagan doctrines and ideas of all sorts are everywhere in vogue."

Simply put, the system of worship as practiced by the Babylonians, Medo-Persians, Greeks and Rome was enforced by Emperor Constantine who was acting as Babylonian High Priest. This was later endorsed by Damasus who took on the position of Babylonian High Priest-Pontiff.

This endorsement enforced the calendar of the Babylonians upon the Church. The Calendar is not the Calendar God gave to us but is that of sun worship which false worship is. This Calendar of worship is the Babylonian system of worship having as its main celebrations Sunday, Christmas and Easter.

Chapter 5: Man's motive for change of systems

We must be clear that at no point did any of the Gospels or Paul's letters ever point to a change in the worship patterns given by God. None of the Christian Festivals, certainly not Sunday, Christmas or Easter are mentioned in Scripture. So who changed them and what was the motive?

Constantine was a military tactician, a supreme political leader and as Babylonian Priest a leader of religious harmony. He managed to meld together three main religions, Mithraism, Isis worship and Christianity.

One of his arguments for doing so was that he was against, what was referred to then and what is referred to now, as Judaism. I want to make it clear that if we are opposed to Judaism we have to throw out the Bible. There is of course biblical and non-biblical Judaism but I am referring to Biblical Judaism. The celebration of Sabbath, seventh day, and Passover is the practice of what Constantine and his Bishops would have referred to as Judaism.

They were, as have been many within Christendom over the centuries, anti-Semitic and therefore opposed to anything connected with Jews. This hatred was not the only motive which led to the forced changes of the worship system. He was in favour of paganism or more directly Mithraism, meaning the worship of the god called the "unconquerable sun."

On 7th March 321 Emperor/Pontiff Constantine issued the following decree regarding Sunday the day of the venerable sun.

"On the venerable day of the sun let the magistrates and the people residing in the cities rest, and let all workshops be closed".

Meaning no work or trade on Sunday but work and trade on Saturday (the day which God gave us to rest- fourth Commandment).

From that time on Sabbath worship was considered a heresy in the Roman Empire and Christendom regarded it as an anathema punishable by death. This meant that those Christians who kept Sabbath and refused to comply with Sunday worship laws implemented by Constantine were executed.

In 325 AD Constantine went on to direct the Bishops at Nicea to enforce the celebration of Easter rather than God's Festival of Passover. This is what the Bishops ordered at that council in Nicea;

"It seems to everyone a most unworthy thing that we should follow the custom of the Jews in the celebration of this most Holy solemnity, who, polluted wretches!, having stained their hands with nefarious crime, are justly blinded in their minds. It is fit therefore, that, rejecting the practice of this people we should perpetuate to all future ages the celebration of this rite, in a more legitimate order. We desire to have nothing in common with this so hated people, for the redeemer has marked out another path for us."

Satan by now, through Constantine and continued through Damasus, had deceived the people and changed God's times, seasons and laws.

These times of worship, which have no bearing whatsoever on God's Festivals and His appointed times of worship, were directly connected to sun worship, and are still practiced today, even amongst those in Christendom who say they have completely broken from Rome.

Christendom is simply continuing with the system of false worship which was established in Babylon. The system was carried through the Babylonian priesthood to Pergamum and later enforced in statute by Constantine and passed on into the Roman Church by Damasus, who took upon himself the mantle of Babylonian High Priest and leader of false worship.

The scriptures and the historic facts have established that there are two systems of worship, one which is God's as given to the Jews to establish on earth as true worship, and a satanic worship system introduced to the world in the form of sun worship which is still practiced today by the majority in Christendom.

Christendom has enforced these changes throughout its history using various councils and dictates, which you will read about later.

The motives are varied and as we look at history we see that they range from a victory of paganism over the Church to antisemitism, hatred of God's laws in favour of men's laws; control in the Church by not allowing others to worship in the way they believe Scripture is telling them they should.

We will read more about this later when we look at Church decrees and political statutes forcing Sunday worship upon Christians.

Chapter 6: The Mark

The next point or principle described by John in Revelation 13 concerns the 'mark', verse 16.

According to the NASB Greek-Hebrew Dictionary the word 'mark' is transliterated 'sign'. As mentioned earlier when God created the lights in the sky it was to be a sign for the Festivals. I also used Strong's to show us that the word sign which has the same root as mark means in the Genesis verse – a 'Divine communication'.

The mark or sign affects all of society, rich, poor, great and small. The mark is to be on the right hand or the forehead. We are therefore looking for a mark or a sign which will deceive all, royals, politicians, lawyers, leaders of all kinds, and ordinary people will carry this mark.

God has shown us in the sky, in scripture and through the ministry of Yeshua the system of worship we should be following. God is communicating with us by His Spirit and God will have those who will tell the world how to worship. What more will people with open hearts to God need? I have shown so many people how they should be practicing their faith, including many Church leaders, and many agree but they refuse to change.

A question you may want to ask ...

At this point my friend asks the question will born again believers be raptured and in heaven before then?

The Scriptures in Daniel chapter 11 v 33 show us that the wise will give understanding to many and so we see that God will have His witnesses on earth as to how to worship and who to worship during this period of the False Messiah who is the Beast in

Revelation 13. God always has witnesses on earth so who will they be at the end of time?

Revelation Chapter 12 v 17 says:

"Then the dragon was angry with the woman, and went off to make war on the rest of her children, those who keep the commandments of God and hold the testimony of Jesus".

This means that "those who keep the commandments of God and hold to the testimony of Yeshua" (who are believers-Jew and Gentile-one new man) will be his target. They have to be here on earth as he cannot target them if they are taken into heaven.

Revelation Chapter 14 verse 12 states that those who keep the commands and testimony of Yeshua, again believers, are called to persevere through these times, meaning they are not gathered but enduring as witnesses. Daniel 11 v 35 says those who are wise will suffer until the time of the end. That means until the return of the Lord.

Another point is that which Paul makes in 1 Thessalonians 4 verses 13 to 17 which is that Yeshua returns with a trumpet call fulfilling the Feast of Trumpets and then the dead who believed will rise, then those who are alive who believe will rise to join them. Those verses make it clear that Yeshua makes one return not two.

In 2 Thessalonians chapter 2 verses 1-12 Paul makes it very clear that the return of The Lord does not come until the False Messiah completes his work. These are the verses:

[1] As to the coming of our Lord Jesus Christ and our being gathered together to him, we beg you, brothers and sisters,

[2] not to be quickly shaken in mind or alarmed, either by spirit or by word or by letter, as though from us, to the effect that the day of the Lord is already here.

[3] Let no one deceive you in any way; for that day will not come unless the rebellion comes first and the lawless one is revealed, the

one destined for destruction.

⁴ He opposes and exalts himself above every so-called god or object of worship, so that he takes his seat in the temple of God, declaring himself to be God.

⁵ Do you not remember that I told you these things when I was still with you?

⁶ And you know what is now restraining him, so that he may be revealed when his time comes.

⁷ For the mystery of lawlessness is already at work, but only until the one who now restrains it is removed.

⁸ And then the lawless one will be revealed, whom the Lord Jesus will destroy with the breath of his mouth, annihilating him by the manifestation of his coming.

⁹ The coming of the lawless one is apparent in the working of Satan, who uses all power, signs, lying wonders,

¹⁰ and every kind of wicked deception for those who are perishing, because they refused to love the truth and so be saved.

¹¹ For this reason God sends them a powerful delusion, leading them to believe what is false,

¹² so that all who have not believed the truth but took pleasure in unrighteousness will be condemned.

Moving back to the mark it has to be clear and conspicuous to the one being worshipped and is, as I have said, on the forehead and right hand. The mark has to be something that the vast majority of people will do willingly as the False Messiah will not want an uprising of the whole world.

If you are a politician or royalty or a world leader I am sure you will not take a physical mark but you would attend religious meetings as prescribed as they do today. We see unbelieving

47

politicians, royalty and leaders attending Christmas and other mainstream services. They just won't realise the spiritual importance of what they are doing.

To explain we must understand the importance of its positioning. We must examine scripture because God would not leave those who have chosen to worship Him guessing.

We first see God saying this sign or mark is to be on the forehead and on the hand when we examine what God says to the Israelites concerning the Torah, and in this case the Festival of Unleavened Bread

"This observance will be for you like a sign on your hand and a reminder on your forehead that the law of the LORD is to be on your lips." Ex 13:9 (ANIV)

When talking about sacrifice which is within the Law and clearly prophetic concerning the sacrifice of Yeshua for the redemption of all who repent and believe, God says;

"It shall be as a sign on your hand and as frontlets between your eyes, for by strength of hand the LORD brought us out of Egypt." Ex 13:16 (NKJV)

The Sabbath is a sign of our obedience to God;

"It will be a sign between me and the Israelites forever, for in six days the LORD made the heavens and the earth, and on the seventh day he abstained from work and rested." Ex 31:17 (ANIV)"

[19] I am the LORD your God; follow my decrees and be careful to keep my laws. [20] Keep my Sabbaths holy, that they may be a sign between us. Then you will know that I am the LORD your God." Ezekiel 20:19-20 (ANIV)

When giving instructions regarding the dress of the High Priest, God commands that he wear a plate on his forehead as follows;

"You shall also make a plate of pure gold and engrave on it, like

the engraving of a signet: HOLINESS TO THE LORD.[37] And you shall put it on a blue cord, that it may be on the turban; it shall be on the front of the turban [38] So it shall be on Aaron's forehead, that Aaron may bear the iniquity of the holy things which the children of Israel hallow in all their holy gifts; and it shall always be on his forehead, that they may be accepted before the LORD." Ex 28:36-38 (NKJV)

In the Jewish Study Bible the word 'frontlet' is used instead of 'plate'. The Strong's Talking Greek & Hebrew Dictionary says that it is from an unused root meaning to go around or bind; a frontlet for the forehead. This word occurs in Exodus 13v16 as we have seen above, Deuteronomy 6v8 and 11v8 which all specifically speak of the Law of God and which state:

"You shall bind them as a sign on your hand, and they shall be as frontlets between your eyes. Deuteronomy 6:8 (NKJV)

"Therefore you shall lay up these words of mine in your heart and in your soul, and bind them as a sign on your hand, and they shall be as frontlets between your eyes." Deuteronomy 11:18 (NKJV)

This is why today we see Jews wearing phylacteries on their head and arms as an outward sign of binding the Torah to the forehead and right arm. Of course the Torah needs to be in our hearts and we need to keep it out of love for God and not as a religious outward sign. Yeshua makes it clear when He is critical of those who do not keep the Torah out of love but out of a religious tradition to 'show off':

"But all their works they do to be seen by men. They make their phylacteries broad and enlarge the borders of their garments." Matthew 23:5 (NKJV)

So we can see clearly that the Laws of God –the patterns and the calendar of worship are a sign or a mark on our foreheads and on our hand between God and His followers. The word forehead has an unused root meaning 'to be clear, i.e. conspicuous; the forehead (as open and prominent).'

We see here that God speaks of the Israelites, who have opposed Gods laws and disobeyed them, as having this as a sign on their forehead and in Ezekiel's case a man who is teaching the truth also has a clear message on his forehead.

"Behold, I have made your face strong against their faces, and your forehead strong against their foreheads. Like adamant stone, harder than flint, I have made your forehead; do not be afraid of them, nor be dismayed at their looks, though they are a rebellious house." Ezekiel 3:8-9 (NKJV)

God knows our hearts and what is in our mind so He knows and sees our keeping His Torah as a sign. So when we celebrate His Festivals and His Sabbath which are His patterns of worship, and we do it out of love for Him, then He sees that as a sign or mark on our foreheads and right arms.

Conversely Satan also sees those who practice his laws and his times as a clear sign or mark on the foreheads and hands of those who follow him and his patterns, which as I have explained are the ancient solar patterns of the invincible day of the sun-Sunday, birth of Mithras-25th December, and the spring equinox celebration of Easter.

Another question!

At this point my friend asked me this question: *"I can't help feeling puzzled about this. I get the impression that even born-again Christians could still be rejected after all, because they did not keep Sabbath and Gods Feasts. After all, they would be wearing the signs of the enemy, having kept Sunday and Christmas etc. But how can God call them 'workers of Lawlessness', when they have sincerely walked with Him?"*

My answer is simple, The Holy Spirit is moving swiftly today across the Christian Church calling born again believers who are really seeking God to return to the Hebrew roots of our faith and to restore the appointed times of The Lord.

For the last fifteen years I have been meeting believers who are hearing The Holy Spirit calling them back to keep the Sabbath and the Feasts. Most of us begin with Passover and then Tabernacles and finally Sabbath. John says 'he who has an ear let him hear'.

If we are true followers then as we hear God and see what He is doing we will follow. I trust God will have His followers and lamp standards at the end of time.

We must remember what we have already said from the book of Hebrews concerning our patterns of worship being a copy of what is happening in the spiritual realm. So for those who say 'Does it matter whether we celebrate Christmas, Easter and Sunday worship?', which is often said to be the Lords Day, then they are not copying Gods' patterns in the spirit realm but Satan's.

I would also respond to this question by saying that theologians across all the denominations would say that there is not a single scripture to support these days.

So there will be those who keep God's commands and believe in Yeshua and these are the ones who will be the target of Satan. I want to point you to the following scriptures which show there is a real connection with the commandments (the Torah), the fourth being seventh day Sabbath, and Yeshua in the end of time;

"And the dragon was enraged with the woman, and he went to make war with the rest of her offspring, who keep the commandments of God and have the testimony of Jesus Christ." Rev 12:17 (NKJV)

"Here is the patience of the saints; here are those who keep the commandments of God and the faith of Jesus."

This is all part of the deception and conditioning by Satan which leads into punishment for those who have the mark of the Beast, which are the false worship patterns.

"And the smoke of their torment ascends forever and ever; and they have no rest day or night, who worship the beast and his

image, and whoever receives the mark of his name." Rev 14:11 (NKJV)

This is how and why all royals, politicians and ordinary people will fall into the trap because it is normal even today to celebrate Sunday, Christmas and Easter- we are conditioned to do so.

Chapter 7: Buying and selling

So what of the question of buying and selling in verse 17?

Will we all have some kind of credit card which is issued so we can only purchase food using that or have a kind of chip on our head so as we enter a supermarket it allows us in? No, of course, as I have explained.

Those who keep to Gods pattern of worship will be well known and ostracised from society, not being able to trade or do business or buy or sell because those who keep to the patterns of Satan and have been deceived into ignoring God's Laws over Satan's will have nothing to do with them. You will be asking now how this can be argued. History gives me masses of evidence to be sure that this is what will happen.

Rev A. H. Lewis, member of the Association of the History of the Church, wrote of Constantine's decree in his book, 'A critical history of Sunday legislation from 321 to 1888', "the pagan religion of Rome had many holidays on which partial or complete cessation of business or labour were demanded, and Constantine by this Sunday Law was merely adding one more festival to the Empire"

The words 'cessation of business' is important as you can see in Revelation 13 v 17.

Dr. A Bang, Lutheran Bishop of Norway, stated in his book 'History of the Christian Church',

"This Sunday law constituted no real favouritism towards Christianity".

Franklyn H Little said:

"It was a triumph of paganism over the Christian movement of the day and it caused the Bishops to serve the state and not the Church and it was bad for the Jews".

Church councils enforced Constantine's pro-pagan anti-Semitic law.

CANON XXIX of the Council of Laodicea in 364 AD said: "CHRISTIANS must not Judaize by resting on the Sabbath, but must work on that day, rather honouring the Lord's Day; and, if they can, resting then as Christians. But if any shall be found to be Judaisers, let them be anathema from Christ".

If you were charged with being anathema you were executed.

As a result millions of Christians throughout history have been slaughtered because they kept the seventh day in honour of God, and legislation regarding buying and selling or trading on a Sunday has been detrimental to them.

Many more Church Councils continued enforcing previous councils. They were enforced in many ways - by deceit, negotiation and persecution including massacre.

The Synod of Whitby, 664 AD is one such example of a community of Christians in the North of England who kept Sabbath and Passover and who were visited by emissaries from Rome and coerced into conforming to the system of worship of Rome.

On the other hand 1200 Christians from Bangor-On-Dee in Wales were slaughtered in one day during the same period because they refused to conform to Roman laws concerning Sabbath and Passover. In fact the Welsh kept the Biblical practice of Sabbath keeping until 1115 AD, and Christians in Ireland and Scotland until 1175.

The Synod of Toulouse in 1163 said:

"The Bishops and Priests are to take care and to forbid under pain of excommunication every person from presuming to give reception, or at least assistance, to the followers of this heresy (Sabbath) whenever they shall be discovered. Neither are they to have dealings with them in buying or selling, that by being thus deprived of the common assistance of life, they may be compelled to repent of the evil of their way"

Church Council in Bergen & Oslo 1435 & 1436 stated:

"It is strictly forbidden - it is stated in The Church Law - for anyone to keep holidays outside of those which the pope, archbishops or bishops appoint". We are informed that some people in different districts of the Kingdom have adopted and observed Saturday keeping. It is severely forbidden. Saturday keeping under no circumstance must be permitted hereafter further that the Church Canon commands. Hereafter we counsel all the friends of God throughout all Norway who want to be obedient towards the Holy Church, to let this evil of Saturday keeping alone, and the rest we forbid under penalty of severe Church punishment to keep Saturday holy.

To try and persuade people to turn away from Saturday, Bishops did all sorts of things including Abbot Eustace 1200 AD who forged a letter which he said was from God to the Church saying;

"I am The Lord.... It is my will, that no one from 9th hour on Saturday (3pm) until sunrise on Monday shall do any work. If you do not pay obedience to this command I swear to you I will rain upon you stones and wood and hot water in the night. Now know that you are saved by the prayers of the most holy mother Mary."

The laws of the Church of Rome are still practiced today even in the Protestant communion and these are the very laws that have caused millions of people to be persecuted, particularly the Waldenses, Insabatita, Cathars, Albigenses, Huguenots, Lollards and many others who were Sabbath keeping communities in

Europe in the middle centuries. They were all persecuted for failing to comply with the Laws instituted by the Roman Church. Decrees were made such as the Decree of King Defonosus of Aragon dated 1194 which stated:

" If any from this day forwards, shall presume to receive into their houses the aforesaid Waldenses and Insabatita, or other heretics, of whatsoever profession they be, or to hear in any place their abominable preaching, or give them food or do them any kind of office whatsoever, let him know that he will incur the indignation of Almighty God and ours, that he shall forfeit all his goods without the benefit of appeal and be punished as though guilty of high treason." (Executed).

In England there were various Acts of Parliament passed to coerce people to attend Church of England services and to prohibit unofficial meetings of lay people, lay people meaning anyone who was not licensed to minister by the Church of England. (Note: The idea of Lay and Clergy was not a practice in the early Church. Paul makes clear in Ephesians 4 v 11-12 that we are all called to minister).

There are a number of Acts of Parliament in Britain concerning conformity to Sunday worship but the following are good examples in the History of English Law.

The Conventicle Act of 1593 allowed for the imprisonment, without bail, of those over the age of sixteen who failed to attend Church on a Sunday, who persuaded others to do the same; who denied Her Majesty's authority in matters of ecclesiastical Laws and who attended unlawful religious conventicles, meaning religious meetings outside that of the Church of England.

The Conventicle Act of 1664 forbade conventicles (religious assemblies of more than five people outside the auspices of the Church of England). This law was part of the Clarendon Code named after Edward Hyde, 1st Earl of Clarendon, which aimed to discourage non-conformism and to strengthen the position of the established Church.

The Conventicle Act of 1670 imposed a fine on any person who attended a conventicle (any religious assembly other than the Church of England) of five shillings for the first offence and ten shillings for a second offence. Any preacher or person who allowed their house to be used as a meeting house for such an assembly could be fined 20 shillings and 40 shillings for a second offence.

The Five Mile Act, or Oxford Act, also known as the Nonconformists Act 1665, was an Act of Parliament for restraining Non-Conformists from inhabiting in Corporations. The act enforced conformity to the established Church of England. It forbade clergymen from living within five miles of a parish from which they had been expelled, unless they swore an oath never to resist the king, or attempt to alter the government of Church or State. This involved swearing an oath to obey the 1662 Book of Common Prayer. Thousands of ministers were punished by this act.

In 1617 John Traske, a Christian Pastor who is better known for his impassioned preaching for all to repent, along with his congregation were arrested for meeting on a Sabbath and not attending the Church of England sacraments on a Sunday. They appeared before the Court of High Commission.

Traske himself was imprisoned so that, as the court said "he may not infect others." In 1618 he was sentenced by the Star Chamber and imprisoned for life. He was fined £1000, whipped from Fleet Prison to Westminster and then to Cheapside. He was also branded on his forehead with the Letter "J" signifying that he was a Judaizer. Traske recanted in 1619 after a year of punishment and a diet of bread and water and was released, but his wife Dorothy remained in prison maintaining the significance of the Sabbath until her death in 1645.

In 1634 an Anglican Minister of Norwich, Theophilus Brabourne, was imprisoned for his writings and teachings about the Sabbath. He was fined £1000, excommunicated from the Church of England and ordered to make a retraction of his views on Sabbath. During his trial it was proposed that the Laws of the 'De heretico comburendo' be brought against him. These were enactments made in 1401 against the Puritans John Wycliffe and the Lollards, who kept Sabbath and other biblical practices and who having translated the Bible into English, were under this act punished by being burnt at the stake. However Brabourne recanted and was spared.

In 1661 John James, a Baptist Pastor at the Baptist Church in Bull Stake Alley, Whitechapel Road, London, was executed in London for his biblical views of the Millennium as described in the book of Daniel and for keeping and teaching the fourth Commandment, namely Sabbath.

At his execution he said "Of the ten commandments as they are expressed in the 20th of Exodus, I do here, as before the Lord, testify I durst not willingly break the least of those Commandments to save my life. I do own The Lord's Holy Sabbath, the seventh day of the week, to be The Lord's Sabbath. You know the command: 'Thou shall keep the seventh day.'"

John James was hung, drawn and quartered and his head was placed on a pole outside the congregation's meeting place at Mill Yard.

Along with all these punishments, buying and selling or what is commonly seen as boycotting, which seems only to be against Israel today and often called for by "the established church", was a common practice throughout Europe against Sabbath keepers. Many communities found themselves unable to buy or sell to other Christian communities, who were afraid to break the laws of Rome and be seen to be aligning themselves with the Sabbath keepers, thereby facing the same punishment.

We must not forget that the Church's attitude towards Sabbath remains strong in its opposition. In America Dr Bascom Robins preached in Burlington Kansas on Sunday 31st January 1904 and said this in regard to buying and selling to those who keep Sabbath:

"In the Christian Decalogue the first day was made the Sabbath by divine appointment. But there is a class of people who will not keep the Christian Sabbath unless they are forced to do so. But that can easily be done. We have twenty million men, besides women and children, in this country who want this country to keep the Christian Sabbath. If we would say we would not sell anything to them, we will not buy anything from them, we will not work for them, or hire them to work for us, the thing could be wiped out and the world would keep the Christian Sabbath."

(You can read more about Sabbath Laws by reading my booklet in the Truth and Clarity series on Legalism).

The outworking of the buying and selling spoken of by John will be easily achieved, as it has been throughout history, simply by the majority in the world who will be worshipping in line with Satan's patterns, refusing to trade with those who keep Gods commands and boycotting them.

The following are just some of the calls for boycotts against Israel in Christendom today which show the extent to which refusing to trade with those who keep to Gods commands could be effective in the final years.

In July 2004, the General Assembly of the Presbyterian Church USA (PCUSA) voted to "initiate a process of phased selective divestment in multinational corporations operating in Israel"

The Church of England Synod has voted for disinvestment from Israel, which was criticised by George Carey as "inappropriate, offensive and highly damaging".

On 5th April 2011 Quakers in Britain agreed to boycott products from the Israeli settlements in the West Bank.

In June 2010, the British Methodist Church decided to begin boycotting products originating in Israeli settlements, becoming the first major Christian denomination in Britain to officially adopt such a policy.

Archbishop Desmond Tutu has called on the international community to treat Israel as it treated apartheid South Africa, and he supports the divestment campaign against Israel.

Swedish Archbishop KG Hammer, Ambassador Carl Tham and a list of 71 others have supported a boycott of products from Israel's 'West Bank'.

Reverend Jim Barr, president of the Australia Palestine Advocacy Network, supports boycott, divestment and sanctions campaigns.

In Australia, the National Council of Churches passed a motion at the end *of July this year backing a boycott of settlement products. The NCCA represents* the Australian branches of the Catholic and Anglican churches, along with 15 other denominations. An NCCA press release states: "We are asking the member Churches of the NCCA to consider boycotting particular goods produced in Israeli settlements in the Occupied Palestinian Territories."

Chapter 8: The number 666

What then of the number 666?

When I hear discussions about the times during which the things that John talks about will take place, I hear the word 'anti-Christ' and reference to the number 666 which makes it all sound very mysterious and 'occultist'.

The fact is that as I have said earlier Satan will disguise himself as a false Messiah who will look like the Messiah to Israel, their Saviour; he will claim to be their deliverer, not an occult figure. The number 666 is not an occult number representing a mysterious evil; it is as John says: a number which, if we know the word of God, will be revealed to us in scripture.

6 is the number of man and stops short of the perfect number 7. Man was created on the sixth day.

Worship of an image is referred to in scripture in the form of the image placed in Dura by Nebuchadnezzar with the number of instruments being 6; it was 60 cubits high and 6 cubits wide.

Nebuchadnezzar the king made an image of gold, whose height was sixty cubits and its width six cubits. He set it up in the plain of Dura, in the province of Babylon. Dan 3:1 (NKJV)

 As soon as you hear the sound of the horn, flute, zither, lyre, harp, pipes and all kinds of music, you must fall down and worship the image of gold that King Nebuchadnezzar has set up. Dan 3:5 (ANIV)

Goliath the oppressor of Gods people was 6 cubits in height; he had six pieces of armour and his spearhead weighed 600 shekels.

[4] *"And there went out a champion out of the camp of the Philistines, named Goliath, of Gath, whose height was six cubits and a span.* [5] *And he had a helmet of brass upon his head, and he was clad with a coat of mail; and the weight of the coat was five thousand shekels of brass.* [6] *And he had greaves of brass upon his legs, and a javelin of brass between his shoulders.* [7] *And the staff of his spear was like a weaver's beam; and his spear's head weighed six hundred shekels of iron: and his shield-bearer went before him."* 1 Sam 17:4-7 (ASV)

We can see that the number 666 represents man. John expected those who have wisdom -Torah understanding, and those with knowledge -Torah keeping followers of Yeshua to understand this. In Christendom today many of us are told not to read 'The Old Testament' despite the fact that John in Revelation quotes from it so often.

How therefore can we have such knowledge and understanding to know what 666 means? We have to read the fullness of the word of God and study it and then we can teach from it as Yeshua, Paul and all the apostles did. We have to be a light for the Word of God so that all will know the number and its meaning. The number is as John says a person and that person is the False Messiah leading false worship in order to deceive the elect. We must ask the question -how has he done so far?

Whose pattern of worship and whose Laws do the majority of worshippers follow today? Clearly it is man's worship calendar, originated in solar worship, ultimately created by Satan himself, and we have been deceived and conditioned to follow blindly his day - the invincible day of the sun, his times and seasons, the birthday of Mithras on 25th December and Easter at the equinox.

These are the marks and signs celebrated by mankind as a clear sign on the forehead and right hand that Satan has established, and he will have his false worship at the most crucial time in the future.

Chapter 9: Conclusion

There is no doubt after a full examination of scripture and history that Sunday and the feasts of the pagans are the Mark of The Beast.

When Yeshua returns however, He will not only bind Satan but will resume strict adherence to the Laws of God which contain the pattern and calendar of true worship, and will establish His Empire - His Kingdom on the earth forever.

"Now have come the salvation and the power and the kingdom of our God, and the authority of his Christ. (True Messiah)" Rev 12:10 (ANIV)

I began by saying that God would not leave us without an answer. John would have expected us to know what he was writing about but today in Christendom we don't seek the word of God and the Prophets to give us an answer, we seek man and our own understanding.

We seek a secular answer to a spiritual question. We think of computer chips, cards and natural identification when we should be seeking spiritual, Divine identifications.

I think Ecclesiastes chapter verses 8:1-6 sums up what I have been trying to say;

[1] Who *is* like a wise *man?* And who knows the interpretation of a thing? A man's wisdom makes his face shine, and the sternness of his face is changed.

[2] I *say,* "Keep the king's commandment for the sake of your oath to God.

[3] Do not be hasty to go from his presence. Do not take your stand

for an evil thing, for he does whatever pleases him."

[4] Where the word of a king *is, there is* power; and who may say to him, "What are you doing?"

[5] He who keeps his command will experience nothing harmful; and a wise man's heart discerns both time and judgment,

[6] Because for every matter there is a time and judgment, though the misery of man increases greatly.

God says; "*My Word is a Lamp unto thy feet*". BUT what do we have on our foreheads and forehands!

~ **Michael Fryer**

Afterword

Many of you will argue that by keeping the Feasts of The Lord we are being religious but it is the opposite way around. We at Father's House enjoy every moment of our calendar of worship and all that it means. Our weekends are such a blessing as we open our Sabbath on a Friday evening.

Since our children were small, we have made the Sabbath a special family time which is what God wants us to do. It has been a time to remember Him and who He is but also to bless our family. We pray for our wives and children, have communion and rest. Then on a Saturday afternoon we have a wonderful lively Spirit filled meeting with our extended Father's House family. We would never change that.

The religious is connected to Sunday as you can see from what I wrote about the Conventicles Act and other restrictions put there by man.

We don't celebrate Christmas with all its pagan paraphernalia and stress. I served as a Police officer and worked over Christmases. What a dreadful time - domestic violence, fighting, murders, drunkenness, abuse, and all leading to massive debt. We now celebrate the Feast of Tabernacles in the autumn. We have fun as God tells us we should in Scripture. We give presents and have lots of family meals with our congregation. We celebrate all the other Feasts as well and they are wonderful times.

If you feel you would like to join us or know more please contact us through our web site www.fathershouse.wales Father's

House Sabbath Congregation is a Christian congregation committed to support Jews in the UK and in Israel. The proceeds from this publication goes to the congregation to help them reach these goals.

The congregation has a programme of educating Christians and the Secular about the biblical mandate for the Jewish people, their history and their future inheritance. This programme takes the form of a seven-module course which has been taught throughout the UK, Eire, Holland, Germany and Lithuania and Belarus.

We are able to train those who would like to become teachers of this programme in their own area. The course has been translated into Dutch and Belarussian. The course has seen some who had antisemitic views such as some members of the British National Party change their opinions entirely. There is clear evidence that education can help prevent hate.

Father's House is very active in its support of Jewish events and advocates for Israel in a number of forums including street advocacy. The Congregation holds Holocaust Exhibitions and helps others to do the same.

If you would like me to come to your area and speak please contact me at Father's House.

If you would like to join us in these and other activities, which are all aimed at reducing hatred in our nation, then please CONTACT US using the details below:

www.FathersHouse.wales

www.facebook.com/fathershousesc

fathershousecongregation@gmail.com

Phone (UK): 01244 823 378

(Int'l): +44-1244 823 378

About the Author

Mike Fryer is a retired National Crime Squad Detective and is currently the pastor of Father's House Sabbath Congregation in North Wales. He is also the founder of Christian for Zion UK.

Mike graduated in Holocaust Studies in 2009, having studied over a period of 4 years at Yad Vashem. He is a regular visitor to Israel, particularly to the southern towns, which are regularly bombarded with rockets from Gaza.

Mike has written a number of booklets to help believers to understand the Feasts, Sabbath and some of the issues surrounding our Christian practice. He also wrote a small book on dealing with the occult and Wiccan practice in Wales. Mike teaches on the Sabbath, the Lord's Feasts, the period of the False Messiah and Christian anti-Semitism including paganism in the Church.

In 2000 Mike wrote the Hidden Treasure Course, a seven session course about Israel which he teaches throughout the UK, Ireland, Europe and Russia, along with a team of instructors. The course is repeated regularly on Revelation TV.

Mike's heart is to help the church find its Jewish identity through education and encouragement and to help all in Christendom understand our past with the aim of preventing the return of the antisemitism/antizionism of old which resulted in the Holocaust amongst other atrocities.

Father's House is a congregation which follows The Lord's Festivals including Sabbath, with passionate worship and a strong emphasis on the word. It also works alongside the Jewish community in both Israel and the UK to build strong relationships.

Other titles by Mike Fryer

ROSE-TINTED MEMORY: HOLOCAUST TRUTHS THAT CAN'T BE ERASED

Discover Christianity's key role in the atrocities of the Holocaust.

Seventy years after the mass murder of the Jews of Europe, Holocaust denial and Holocaust revisionism are creeping into our overall perception of what actually happened.

The truth is this: Christendom not only fueled the hatred of Jews prior to the war years, but it actually played an active role in intensifying hatred against the Jews of Europe.

This book highlights a number of events which will help you to form more accurate conclusions about the involvement and motives of Christians in Europe in the years surrounding World War II.

Faced with a clearer and more accurate perspective, you will be challenged to take the next step and actively get involved in setting the record straight in our day.

Search for "**Rose-tinted Memory**" on Amazon in both paperback and Kindle versions.

Printed in Great Britain
by Amazon